M000085249

RITA

Ellen Devlin

Červená Barva Press
Somerville, Massachusetts

Červená Barva Press
P.O. Box 440357
W. Somerville, MA 02144-3222

www.cervenabarvapress.com

Bookstore: www.thelostbookshelf.com

Photograph and cover design by Hugh Scully

ISBN: 978-1-950063-13-0

ACKNOWLEDGMENTS

With thanks to the editors who published my poem, in a slightly different form:
Poet Lore: "So Far to Gather in My Hair," Fall/Winter 2013.

Sources

Baltimore Catechism No. 2. Project Gutenberg, 2005, http://www.gutenberg.org/cache/epub/14554/pg14554.html. Accessed 8 June 2016.

Bronte, Emily. *Wuthering Heights*. Dover Publications, 1996.

Chopin, Kate. *The Awakening*. Herbert S. Stone and Co., 1899.

Gilman, Charlotte Perkins. "The Yellow Wallpaper." *Charlotte Perkins Gilman Reader*, edited by Ann J. Lane, Pantheon Books, 1980.

Hawthorne, Nathaniel. *The Scarlet Letter*. Wisehouse Classics, 2015.

James, Henry. *The Golden Bowl*. C. Scribner, 1904.

James, Henry. *Portrait of a Lady*. Viking, 1996.

Tolstoy, Leo, *Anna Karenina*. Dover Publications, 2004.

Wharton, Edith. *The House Of Mirth*. C. Scribner's Sons, c1933.

With thanks to my family, for your love and
encouragement, my teachers and fellow poets for the how
and why of poetry.
Thanks to my brother, Hugh, for keeping my chin up.

With thanks to Červená Barva Press for publishing *RITA*

TABLE OF CONTENTS

For C, who has always been with me

RITA

Border

I lived in a house
next to the little girl
from the red-brick
ivy-thick apartment.

The alley between us
was a sweet stillness
of bluestone slate, dark
in day, collateral
for an old argument—

one foundation wall poured
five feet from the other.

We examined everything
always looking
for someone
to blame for the loss
of light. How can people
who have nothing give up
the warm weight of grievance,
the way it fills their pockets?

I stopped speaking
to the little girl
who stretched her finger
through the fence
to give me a caterpillar.

She yelled something
I don't remember,
and I threw a stone
at her small, pale forehead.

Rita Remembers her Grandmother

Her name was Missouri and that's what I called her.
She drank Johnny Walker Red from a tea cup
and ate oatmeal that was so cold it fell from the pot
still holding the shape of it. My family had crucifixes
and Sacred Heart pictures. You know the ones
with his shirt open and flames shooting from his heart?
She had a picture of Franklin Delano Roosevelt
with a brass bowl and waxed fruit placed before it.
I was an altar. She said FDR did more discernible good
than Jesus ever did. She was the only woman I knew
who read four newspapers. Three of her children died
before they could go to school. She said of herself,
this is what comes of a small life with a mean-spirited man.
Oh Missouri, I am lost and rummaging through you
looking for a sign.

Rita on Desire

Do you remember growing a body
with an electrical charge that rivaled lightening?
How you curved and curled into another's hollows
and left park grass singed beneath you, hiss and steam,
light shining from the spaces between your teeth?

Now I hardly remember the sound of desire.
It's a pillowed hammer, soft, without insistence.

Rita Reassures Hester Prynne
after *The Scarlet Letter*

Adultery can be a luminous sin,
ordinary as flashlight in a dark cellar.
We find the trunk with the notebook
with our plans, numbered. We forget
the taste of put-up apples
after so many winters. A new love
makes us dust off the tin dollhouse
and weep at the plastic chairs, so perfect.

Rita on the Sin Set-Up

All gods are arsonists. They are the fire.
They set them in our bodies. Tease out
the old romance movie thing: sleepy lovers
let a lit cigarette fall. The whole sin cycle,
crime and punishment, done in a few hours
of desire/death by fire. The penance
so satisfying to the jehovahs—
we do the whole thing ourselves. We are made
in the image and likeness. We think
with the brain we got: itchy body
or peaty whisky? If you were god, could you
laugh off the failed experiment, engineer
the software so we could not desire/
set fire to ourselves and others?

Rita Edits *The Baltimore Catechism*

Who is god?
God is earth, woman, man,
A beginning, everywhere.
All things are infinitely perfect.
Create heaven and earth
By a single act, woman and man.
Eat blessings.
Eat all that is forbidden.
We are original goodness,
Innocent and holy.
All wombs are blessed.
Hearts are merciful and peacemaking.
Ruling passion is holy, brilliant—
True tongue of fire.
This is my body, this is my blood.
We are the messengers, sacred dispensers,
Interpreters of mystery, worthiness itself.
All water is holy.
Heretics and infidels are thy neighbor.
Hallowed be their names.
The fullness of creation is not yet in the world.
The exact place of the Garden of Eden is known.
It's here, on earth.

Rita Remembers the Social Worker

I was five, and my mother was gone.
A woman with a brown coat
and a hat with a big feather
was talking to me.

Her words, tiny, cold meteors
had no heat or velocity.
I was looking at her shoes, mine.
Our four shoes looked at a single
black suede high heel
lying on its side
on the bottom landing.

I saw this: night, three men
pulling my mother down the stairs,
she was arching her back into a corner,
feet planted, quiet.
Her shoe fell off.

It sounded like a small animal,
a rabbit, or a bird,
falling ahead of her
down the stairs.

I felt a ghost child
move out from me.
She looked just like me
and she looked, too,
at my mother's shoe.

Rita at the Supermarket

This place is a white tile wasteland with a florescent unsky.
I could be a prophet waiting for divine direction,
especially because I don't want it.
God seems to like the unwilling.
It's easy to corner us among sour smell mops
and bruised apricots while we are distracted
by odd-looking shoppers like the big man
I see sometimes wearing a red skirt, long and billowy,
tee shirt and black boots. I wonder if he feels
unready to be called too as he pushes his cart
filled with canned tomatoes, glassed-in honey.

Rita Talks Back to Anna Karenina
after Anna Karenina

Look at you, laid on a table, a shattered-fruit body,
your hair slick with blood. What was proved
by throwing yourself under a train? Any life is better.
A glass of tea, cold, the bite and bruise
of any day is better. Those men who pushed
your exploded bones into a body-shape
under your dress are home now, eating potatoes
and onions and smiling at their ugly wives.

Rita Talks Back to Ellen Oleska
after *The Age of Innocence*

You think you're going somewhere, Countess?
Look around you. Even the walls insist
on constriction. Look at the painting—
silver starlings in flight carry berry branches
in their clamped tight beaks. Beautiful birds
with blue ribbons on their necks, flying in cages.

Rita Talks Back to Maggie Verver
after The Golden Bowl

The Bowl is gilded glass
with a fissure in its intention
to be a bowl.

The prince is a bridegroom
with a fracture his body chooses.

His abandoned lover leaves herself.
Everyone else hides

And you all eat together
from this impossible china, nightly?

Rita at the Riverton Library Book Club

I suggested Ethan Frome. I'm tired of wedding stories set
    in Cape Cod
and talking about experiences with lobsters,
unworthy men.

I wish the club wanted to hear the voices from frozen
graveyards, impenetrable spruces,
so I'd have someone to talk to about it.

Light is brought to our brains by bleakness
howling like a Russian night.

Despair is a precious poison inoculating us from ourselves.

Must every message brought back from hell,
be carried by the one sister who isn't jealous,
who eats the sorrow of an unworn dress?

Rita Waits on the Stoop for her Lover

He said he would come get me at noon.
I think it's past noon. Baby strollers have all wheeled home
from the one-tree, one-swing park. All the old men
left the deli with their sandwiches wrapped in white paper.
He'll be here soon, his arm resting
on the window rim of his Volvo.

I put waxed paper in the bottom of the bag
so the blood wouldn't leak out on the steps. A woman
walks by with a spaniel, sniffing his way up the stairs
and now he's on his hind legs, barking,
yanking the leash towards me. He's going for the bag,
the tiny chicken heart in it, so I pull it back
from his blue tongue slick with saliva.

I always carry the paper bag with me now,
to remind me of how easily I ignore betrayal.
I read in National Geographic about a man
who was found in a bog. He'd been floating
in the mud, clubbed and throat-slit for 1,800 years.
The article said he was a willing victim, and in his stomach
was a scorched grain cake.

Rita Reads the Court Documents

My mother's eyes were brown
and sometimes empty.

The involuntary admission report said
a young white woman, sleep

and appetite disturbed, weepy.
She does not do her work.

In the photograph
she is smiling, her lips

pulled into a taut line.
But the corners

of her mouth
and her brown eyes lift.

That's her smile that
always said *finally.*

I smile back at her
every time I see it.

Rita Talks Back to Catherine Earnshaw
after *Wuthering Heights*

He was no great love. Your life was haunted
from the start by want of space, food, reason—
Doors locked without a key for your pocket.
When you pushed a broom across the floor
over and over, you heard it whisper suffers, suffers.

Where women walk unlit hallways of home,
their hands ache and twist to hold, what?
We pry at the closed fist of rotted fruit
looking for sweetness.
Fierce hungers breed fierce attachment.
Then do you, as I, make a lover of a cruel fury,
a drunk? All are starved. All are stunted.

Rita Warns Lily Bart
    after *The House of Mirth*

Be careful, Lily, your dread runs
wet and uneasy down men's shirts.
Use your humor, wear your best.
Lighthearted indifference is the way
with men with money. Smile—
place a wide table between your craving
for ease and their fear of your lingering.
Someone will take you in.

Rita Remembers Herself at Seven

The kitchen pantry was tall and narrow,
winter-dark, cold-walled,
mice scratching between cereal boxes.
A small window held a white dot moon.
It was a silver spill on the window ledge,
a milk promise, pulling me.
I went to see that moon melt on dirty glass, every night,
even when a flag pulled by a plane through daylight sky
     said:
you eat the same food as mice.

Rita Contacts Customer Service

Thank you for fast-tracking
the delivery of my necklace. But
when I put it on, it moves about one inch
from the center of my body to the right.
I think it's because the metals used
under the gold plating are connected
to the pull of gravity from the moon
or attracted by planetary singing,
or some other force described by physics.
I don't understand physics and
I don't know how a pendant
can make me ignore a roomful of Arbus photos
to look at myself in the glass instead
and keep checking if the pendant has returned to center.
I can't wear it and I can't leave it in a drawer.
I get up at night and put it back on and it is still skewed.
I am returning it with no wish for another,
you can return my money to the original source
of payment, maybe cleanse it with salt and bury it.

Rita Works on her Closet

I emptied it. It's a pile of ideas
about being seen/not seen.
Who wants my confusion, my fake fur?
If I knew what to keep and what to give away,
there would be no need to empty.
I want to write on the care labels *desire is endless*.
I threw away all my reproduction art posters
and two days later, weeping,
pulled them from a dumpster. I gave my umbrella
to a rain-soaked woman at a bus stop,
her relief almost as terrible as my regret.

Rita Warns Isabel Archer
after *Portrait of a Lady*

Isabel, do you see the narrowing,
see him putting lights out, one by one?
Lean back in your chair. Listen to his words—
You have too many ideas and must get rid of them.

Rita Talks to the Unnamed Woman
after "The Yellow Wallpaper"

The flowers do seem to move
in the sub-pattern of leaves.
I can see the eyes in the paper, too—
the sulfur got to them. I can feel it.

The yellow smell hides in my hair,
yours. He put you in here
because of the paper. You see that,
don't you? It smothers
even our want to tell someone.

So many women, creeping.

Rita Just Listens to Edna Pontellier
after The Awakening

My days are full of drowning. Women
scold with the soft face of rose mallow,
and water slips between my teeth.
Words stick to my lips and tongue,
tangle in the dead fish
at the bottom of a Louisiana summer.
I am beyond where I can save myself.
The water covers my head, and my held breath
yanks my jaw open. The Gulf floods my lungs.
I hear my father's voice, wind worrying
loosestrife, the hum of bees.

Rita Remembers August, 1966

I am 15 and late, told to be home
by 10 from the three-table pizza place,
and I can't believe my hair isn't frizzing
in the humid night or the guy I watched
all summer broke up with his much prettier
girlfriend and he is here lighting Marlboros
for me. There were still jukeboxes in August, 1966
playing songs over the fear of having no idea
what happens under a lifted skirt. I'm leaving
with the guy to find out, and my father
is in the doorway, tired-eyed. He points to me
and jerks his thumb over his shoulder.
He holds the door open with his hip
All the sidewalk-bound trees are watching.
I am a small animal. It doesn't matter
that he is not always bad-tempered, I
have small animal ways of appeasing.
He doesn't say anything as he drives.
The windows and doors are locked, and I can feel
my mother's life barreling towards me.

ABOUT THE AUTHOR

Ellen Devlin's poetry has been published or is forthcoming in *The Cortland Review*, *Ekphrasis*, *Lime Hawk Review*, *PANK*, *The New Ohio Review*, *The Sow's Ear* and *Women's Studies Quarterly Review*. One chapbook is forthcoming from Červená Barva Press, "Heavenly Bodies at the MET." She lives in Irvington, New York, with her husband, Charles.

CPSIA information can be obtained
at www.ICGtesting.com
Printed in the USA
LVHW040250011019
632709LV00005B/610/P